Introduction   2

W9-APR-405

Introduction

We have written this book to help you find safer personal care items, foods, toys, clothing, bedding and other household products for your baby. We provide simple guidelines that show you what to look for and what to avoid. We explain how chemical ingredients can be harmful and why babies and young children are more vulnerable. From the nursery to the kitchen, you will find the information you need to make your entire home safer. For more in-depth information, we include listings of books, websites, and other resources on these topics.

Why the need for this book?

Unlike any other time in human history, our world is filled with hundreds of thousands of synthetic chemicals, most of which are petro-chemicals (petroleum-based). With over 1,000 new chemicals introduced each year into our environment and food chain, the potential for harm is staggering.

In an attempt to keep the public informed, there is a constant barrage from the media about the dangers of chemicals and additives in seemingly everything. This includes the foods we eat, the products we put on our skin, cleaning products, insect repellents, carpeting, and even plastic baby bottles. No one can tell you with certainty whether these newly introduced chemicals are harmless or harmful. **Reports of safety concerns can be confusing. This book will help you to find and use safer options and explain why it's worth your time to do so.**

Aren't chemicals in home products tested for safety?

Most people assume that ingredients in personal care and household products have undergone intense safety testing before reaching the consumer. Sadly, the truth is, they do not. The startling reason: **There are no governmental requirements for the safety testing of chemicals used in these products.** Companies are encouraged to conduct voluntarily safety testing, but most do not.* Furthermore, claims made by companies on product safety and effectiveness are not evaluated by governmental agencies. The laws are biased to protect industry and not the health and safety of consumers. This results in a reactionary system of regulation that occurs only after health problems have occurred.

> **A TYPICAL SCENARIO:** Untested chemicals are used in the manufacturing of a product, the product is used by millions of consumers, health problems occur, and only then is safety research conducted. Years later, after a class-action lawsuit, the government reacts with a safety recall, ban, and/or warning label. In the meantime, millions of people have been exposed to the harmful chemicals in the product.**

This scenario is similar to the actual product use record for many substances that are now known to be toxic. These include lead in paint and gasoline, arsenic in wooden playground sets, asbestos in insulation, PCBs in transformers, and many of the chemicals found in pesticides. **Governmental regulations for reduction/removal of these toxic substances occurred only after they caused serious health problems.**

* GAO Report, June 2005 (gao.gov)
** Updates on safety testing and recalls: fda.gov, epa.gov, recalls.gov, cpsc.gov

What can we do now?

While we wait for better government regulations, companies to "do the right thing," or for independent scientific testing, is there something we can do now? The answer is YES! Each of us can learn which products are safer choices and how to avoid chemicals that may cause problems. **This effort is especially important to protect babies and young children who are at increased risk for health problems due to exposure to harmful chemicals.**

Learning to select safer products in order to reduce exposure to toxins is easier than you may think. For example, simple products such as baking soda and vinegar are effective cleaners and are safer than commercially prepared cleaners that contain synthetic and/or toxic chemicals. **When safe, natural substances are not available, we provide guidelines to help you choose which ingredients to look for and which to avoid.** Greater use of and demand for safer products by consumers will result in both improvements in health and increased availability of safer, non-toxic products.

I. *Getting Started*

Before we describe how chemicals get into the body (*Body Facts*, page 8) and how to decipher product ingredients (*Learning About Ingredients,* page 12), we begin with the following guidelines. To get started, we suggest applying these guidelines to one or two areas of concern (such as the nursery, food, or cleaning products). As you gain confidence making safer choices, it will become second nature to apply them to all of the products in your home.

- **Look for <u>WARNING LABELS</u>. A warning label is a tip-off that a product has safety issues**. A Warning, Caution or Danger label is not voluntary. Such labels are placed on a product when required by a government safety regulation, usually after the product caused harm. In other words, it is likely that one or more of the ingredients in the product caused serious human injury or death. **After reading the safety concerns, you may decide to find another product with safer ingredients.** We especially urge you to consider non-toxic options for pest, weed and flea/tick control (page 45) and cleaning products (page 28).

- **Product instructions are important and should always be followed carefully for correct (safer) product use.** This is especially true of products with Warning, Caution, or Danger labels.

- **Take the time to read ingredients lists.** The length and complexity of a list of ingredients is often an indication of unsafe ingredients, i.e., **simple is often safer**. Don't let long words or chemical names intimidate you. Using our lists and guidelines in *Learning About Ingredients*, you can become familiar with ingredient names and learn to avoid the common offenders with minimal time and effort.

- **There is no government requirement that personal care and household products be tested for safety before reaching the consumer.** Thus, even if a product has no Warning, Caution, or Danger label, it may contain chemicals that cause harm. Choose products with complete lists or full disclosure of ingredients. This allows you to get safety data on each ingredient. On page 15, we list specific ingredients that are questionable yet do not carry warning labels and provide web resources to look up safety information on any ingredient (e.g., cosmeticsdatabase.com).

- **Be aware that there is no governmentally approved "safety label."** Although products labeled "environmentally friendly" or "green" may be safer, there is no standard for earning such a label. Further, safety claims have been rescinded for a number of ingredients. This occurred for DEET, an insect repellent ingredient. After several children were debilitated or died from repeated exposure to DEET, the Environmental Protection Agency (EPA) ruled to remove child safety claims for DEET on product labels. Unless an ingredient has a long research record for safety, use caution and find out more about the ingredient rather than assume it is safe.

- **We advise caution when using plastics** for food and beverages and for products that could be chewed on by children. Plastics exposed to heat, sunlight, microwaves and strong cleansers tend to leach chemicals which some research has found to affect human health. More information on plastics can be found on pages 21, 22, 39 and 40.

- **Products with strong odors generally present problems**. When strong fumes/odors are inhaled they can have a toxic effect by gaining entry to the bloodstream and brain (see *Body Facts)*. Strong fumes can trigger asthmatic attacks, headaches, dizziness, mental confusion, nausea, etc.

- **If you must use a harsh chemical for cleaning or home projects, always use it with maximum ventilation.** The EPA has estimated indoor air to be 7 to 100 times more polluted than outdoor air. Simply opening a window can dramatically improve indoor air quality. However, exhaust fans and other means of increasing airflow and air purification are also strongly recommended when using any substance with strong fumes. If you use harsh chemicals such as paint thinner, varnish, adhesives, solvents or bleach, do so outdoors whenever possible.

- **Many newly manufactured products contain harmful chemicals called volatile organic compounds (VOCs).** VOCs include formaldehyde and a variety of petroleum-based solvents and are commonly found in new products such as carpeting, wood furniture, office equipment, paneling, composite wood products, and plastics products such as new computers, phones, TVs, and furniture. **VOC fumes emitted or "out-gassed" into the air from these products can cause acute and chronic health problems.** Therefore, they need "airing out" or to be placed in a room with maximum ventilation before closed-room use. Guidelines for "airing out" an item vary (weeks to months), but any detectable odor from a product is likely to be a problem.

II. *Body Facts*

Most people unknowingly expose their children and themselves to hundreds of chemicals in household and personal care products on a daily basis. Understanding how chemicals get into the body and how the body reacts will help you identify and choose safer options.

Are harmful chemicals really getting into our bodies?

Recent research shows that hundreds of chemical toxins are found in the blood and urine of both children and adults who do not exhibit health problems. These findings demonstrate that we have all been exposed to toxins and are storing them in our bodies. The long-term consequences of this chemical "body burden" are not completely understood, but recent reports document at least 180 human health problems associated with toxins. **These disorders include: childhood brain cancer, childhood leukemia, breast, prostate, testicular and ovarian cancers, seizure disorders, attention deficit disorders, diabetes, asthma, and even psychiatric disorders including anxiety, depression and mood disorders.**[*]

[*]Sources: http://database.healthandenvironment.org   healthychild.org   chem-tox.com/pesticides
chemicalbodyburden.org   ewg.org   beyondpesticides.org
environmentalnews.org   loe.org   childenvironment.org

Environmental Toxicants and Developmental Disabilities. S. M. Koger, T. Schettler and B. Weiss. *American Psychologist* 60 (3) 243-255, 2005.

The Right Start: The Need to Eliminate Toxic Chemicals from Baby Products. Oct, 2005 USPIRG Education Fund. Online at: http://safefromtoxics.org/reports/therightstart.pdf

Trends in Environmentally Related Childhood Illnesses. T. Woodruff et al. *Pediatrics* 113(4) 1133-1140, 2004.

How chemicals get into the body:

- Chemicals found in household and personal care products can enter the body through the skin (including scalp), mouth, eyes and nose (inhaled into lungs and absorbed into nasal passages).

- Once a chemical enters the body, it may enter the bloodstream or bodily organs, including the lungs and brain. **In pregnant women, these chemicals can then cross the placenta, and in lactating women can enter breast milk.** Nonetheless, most medical experts agree that the benefits of breastfeeding outweigh the potential risk (nrdc.org/breastmilk).

- **Breathing in airborne chemicals** (such as perfume/cologne, air fresheners, harsh cleaners and other fragranced products) is the fastest way these toxins get into the bloodstream and to the brain. **Acute symptoms of exposure to toxic airborne chemicals** include: headache, nausea, dizziness, migraines, asthma, wheezing, coughing, behavioral/mood changes (such as irritability, depression), fatigue, flu-like symptoms, mental confusion, and/or memory problems.

- **Volatile organic compounds (VOCs)** can easily gain access to the blood and brain through inhalation or via skin contact. Most harmful VOCs have strong odors and are found in products such as oil-based paints, solvents, nail polish, nail polish remover, glues, markers, fragrances, perfumes, colognes, and even scented candles. For more on VOCs, see pages 34 and 37. "Out-gassing" fumes are also emitted from new products such as wood, composite or plastic furniture, carpeting, building materials, and hard plastics (e.g., computers, phones, TVs). **We recommend using maximum ventilation with these products, finding VOC-free or low-VOC substitutes, or avoiding them altogether.**

Additional facts regarding chemicals and health:

- **The liver is the main organ that "detoxifies" or removes harmful chemicals from the bloodstream.** Some people have an inborn (genetic) decrease in liver functioning (such as lower liver enzymes) making them more sensitive and susceptible to the effects of harmful chemicals. This partially explains why some people exhibit more sensitivity to toxins than others.

- **Certain vitamins, minerals and herbs can improve liver functioning and/or help protect the rest of the body from toxins.** Examples: Both vitamin C and milk thistle (an herb) can improve liver functioning; an adequate calcium intake can reduce lead absorption into bone.

- **Stress, poor nutrition, prior disease, alcohol/drug/medication abuse, and previous/ongoing exposure to chemicals can impair the liver's ability to remove toxins from the body.** However, such impairments can be improved or reversed. Certain herbal supplements can help cleanse the liver and other organs from toxins as well as improve immune system functioning.*

- **Dieting and hormonal changes (such as with pregnancy, breast feeding and menopause) can release stored toxins into the bloodstream.** Getting the appropriate levels of vitamins and minerals can help protect you during these vulnerable times.*

- **For information on chemical exposure and health, see page 53.**

* Seek a qualified health care practitioner who is knowledgeable about the value of vitamins, minerals and herbs for recommendations on supplements for your entire family.

Why children are more vulnerable to harmful chemicals:

- A child's smaller size and weight result in a higher dose (amount of chemical per body weight) compared to an adult.

- A child is more vulnerable because body systems such as the nervous, immune and hormonal systems are in critical stages of development. **Starting even in the first trimester of pregnancy, exposure to toxins during critical developmental stages has been shown to have lifelong health consequences.**

- **The liver is the most important organ for removing toxins from the blood (detoxifying). However, a child is more vulnerable to toxins because his or her liver is not yet fully mature and is incapable of functioning as well as an adult's liver**. Exposure to toxins is magnified during prenatal development, infancy and early childhood because toxins stay in body systems longer and at higher concentrations compared to adults.

Note on mercury: Because a child's liver is immature and cannot effectively remove toxins, we recommend parents insist on **preservative-free vaccines** (i.e., mercury/thimerosal-free and phenol-free). For more on mercury exposure, see healthychild.org, safeminds.org and 909shot.com. For safety guidelines on mercury in seafood, see page 24.

Note on fluoride: See fluoridealert.org and ewg.org for the health risks associated with fluoridated water and for more information on fluoride in other products. Given the potential health risks of fluoride, we recommend filtering drinking water with added fluoride.

III. *Learning About Ingredients*

The key to selecting safer products is to know about their ingredients. Here are some tips:

- **READ THE LABEL carefully. Look for products labeled "all-natural" or "organic"** but read further to see how these terms are defined. While neither term guarantees that a product is free of harmful chemicals, it is a good place to start. We recommend that if the label says "organic", you should also look for a ***USDA Certified Organic*** or ***Quality Assurance International-Certified Organic*** label. This labeling indicates that at least 95% of the product ingredients were grown or raised without the use of synthetic fertilizers, synthetic pesticides (herbicides, insecticides, fungicides), antibiotics, growth hormones, irradiation, genetically modified organisms (GMOs), or sewage sludge. See ams.usda.gov/nop for more.

- **Avoid synthetic ingredients,** often with long unfamiliar chemical names or abbreviations. We advise this not only for baby's personal care products, but also for make-up that a baby may have exposure to from skin contact, inhalation or via breast milk. Most skin cream, foundation, eye shadow, lipstick, nail polish, etc. contains unsafe chemicals that gain access to the body through the skin, eyes, nose and/or mouth. **Safer, non-toxic personal care products and make-up are available.** Choose products with safer ingredients listed on page 18 and avoid the ingredients listed on page 15. See page 62 for companies and websites that sell safer products and cosmeticsdatabase.com to find safety ratings for personal care/make-up ingredients and products.

- **Note the order of listed ingredients**. Ingredients in personal care and food products are listed in order from the greatest amount (listed first) to the least amount (listed last), i.e., a product contains *less* of the ingredient listed *last* on a label compared to the ingredient listed *first.*

- **Although simpler is often safer, there are important exceptions**. Examples of simple ingredients to avoid are mineral oil and talc (see page 19). Conversely, some beneficial ingredients have longer names (e.g., d-alpha tocopheryl acetate is a form of natural vitamin E). When in doubt, see page 58 for ways to do web searches on questionable ingredients.

- **Avoid products with "fragrance," "perfume," "scent" or "masking fragrance" as ingredients. This includes perfumes, colognes, after-shaves and body sprays.** Unless stated otherwise, fragrances are made up of combinations of harmful VOCs that gain access to the brain and bloodstream through the nose, skin or mouth (see *Body Facts*). These chemical combinations or "trade secret" formulas are made up of diluted levels of ingredients known to be highly toxic in greater amounts. Few, if any, of these ingredients have undergone safety testing to rule out harmful effects, especially to developing children. This also applies to scented products such as carpet fresheners, spray/plug-in air fresheners, spray "odor removers", dryer sheets, laundry detergents, fabric softeners, household cleaners and scented candles/oils. For more, see www.ehnca.org and fpinva.org. Safer alternatives to perfume and scented products are unscented (fragrance-free) products or those containing pure plant-based essential oils as scent ingredients. Note that most essential oils are too strong for babies; see footnote on page 18.

Ingredients to Avoid or Minimize in Personal Care Products or Processed Foods

The following page is a list of ingredients commonly found in baby personal care products and/or in processed foods. We recommend avoiding or at least minimizing exposure to these ingredients. While these chemical ingredients may make products more convenient to use, "better" looking/smelling/tasting or less likely to spoil, each has a known or suspected health concern.

We recommend using the list on the following page when you shop. To find more information on specific health concerns for these and other chemical ingredients, see the footnote on the next page and references/websites in *How to Learn More.*

INGREDIENTS TO AVOID (OR MINIMIZE) *	ALSO KNOWN OR LISTED AS *
artificial flavors/FD&C or D&C colors	flavoring/coloring
artificial sweeteners (e.g., aspartame, sucralose)	"sugar-free", "reduced-sugar"
BHA, BHT, nitrates, nitrites, sodium/potassium benzoate	preservatives, natural preservatives
cocamide DEA	
cocamidopropyl betaine	
disodium or tetrasodium EDTA	
fluoride, sodium fluoride	sodium monofluorophosphate
fragrance, perfume	scent, parfum, aroma
hydantoin (MDM or DMDM)	formaldehyde, formalin
isopropyl, butyl, benzyl, stearyl, or SD-40 alcohols	
MEA, DEA, or TEA (mono, di or triethanolamine)	ethanolamine
methylparaben, propylparaben, butylparaben	methylparahydroxybenzoate, etc.
mineral oil, petrolatum, petroleum jelly	baby oil
MSG (monosodium glutamate), hydro/autolyzed protein/yeast	flavor enhancer, yeast extract, torula yeast
PEG (polyethylene glycol), PG (propylene glycol)	propylenglycolum
quaternium-15, polyquaternium	methenamine
SLS, ALS (sodium or ammonium lauryl sulfate)	laureth, laurel (SLES)
sodium borate/tretraborate	boric acid
talc, magnesium silicate	talcum powder
triclosan	antibacterial
urea(s) with prefixes	midazolidinyl

* For information on potential health problems for these and other questionable ingredients see:
cosmeticsdatabase.com   lesstoxicguide.ca   cspinet.org   healthychild.org

Household Products with the Most Toxic Ingredients:

Pesticides
insecticides
weed killers
lawn chemicals
flea/tick products

Harsh Cleaners
bleach, ammonia, lye, etc.

VOCs and Volatile Solvents
paint thinner, glue, etc. (see pages 9 & 34)

The importance of correct use, storage and disposal of these products cannot be overemphasized. While most of these products do have Danger, Caution and/or Warning labels, their use is not restricted and they are often used improperly or carelessly.

Even with these warning labels, people assume "they must be safe" because these household products are widely available for purchase. This is simply not true. **Childhood leukemia, brain tumors, learning disabilities, brain damage, depression, hyperactivity, impulsivity, and asthma are among the health problems that have been linked to early childhood exposure to these common household chemicals.*** We provide more information on these toxic products as well as safer options in **Cleaning Products** and **Around the Home**, with additional sources in *How to Learn More*.

* childenvironment.org healthandenvironment.org loe.org
healthychild.org chem-tox.com/pesticides ewg.org

IV. *Home and Personal Care*

Baby Personal Care Products

Choosing safer personal care products is especially important for infants because their skin is immature, thinner and more porous. This results in a greater body burden from chemicals applied topically compared to older children and adults. From baby shampoo to diaper cream, finding safer baby products without synthetic, petroleum-based chemical ingredients is easier than you might think. We list some of the companies that make safer baby personal care products on page 62. Many of these product lines are available online, at natural foods stores such as Whole Foods Market®, Wild Oats® Natural Markets, Earth Fare®, and at local/regional health food stores and natural food co-ops (see page 65). Safer products may also be found in the natural sections in some major grocery stores.

When looking for safer products, the most important thing is to **READ THE INGREDIENTS LIST**. Look for products labeled "natural" or "organic" (see page 12 for organic definition). Neither of these terms guarantees that a product is free of harmful chemicals, but it is a good place to start. After a little practice, it will take only a moment to determine whether a product's ingredients are natural or artificial, safe or potentially harmful. When shopping, use the list of natural ingredients and products on the next two pages to make safer choices. Refer to page 15 for ingredients to avoid or minimize.

SAFER NATURAL INGREDIENTS FOR BABY'S PERSONAL CARE*
(choose organic wherever possible)

Botanical Oils: jojoba, almond, coconut (not sodium laurel sulfate), olive, apricot kernel, avocado, safflower, palm, evening primrose, borage, babassu, etc.

Herbal Extracts******:** such as calendula (used in natural diaper rash cream)

Vitamins: vitamin A (retinyl palmitate), carotene (pro-vitamin A), B vitamins/pro-vitamins (e.g., pantothenic acid, panthenol, inositol, biotin), vitamin C (ascorbic acid), vitamin E (tocopherol or d-alpha tocopheryl in natural form)

Natural Preservatives: vitamins A, C, and E, grapefruit seed extract, citric acid and other antioxidants

Soap (bar or liquid): vegetable glycerin or castile (from natural plant oils, diluted/mild formula)

Other Natural Ingredients: aloe vera, vegetable glycerin, shea butter, mango butter, kokum butter, beeswax, soya lecithin

* For more information, check out the Natural Ingredients Dictionary at aubrey-organics.com and other safer ingredients and options at lesstoxicguide.ca. See cosmeticsdatabase.com for ingredient safety ratings of personal care products.

**Pure essential oils and herbal extracts are fine for adult products, but may be too strong for babies. We also note that some essential oils (e.g., lavender, tea tree) affect hormone levels and are therefore not appropriate for children. For safe use of essential oils and herbal extracts, consult a certified herbalist.

Baby Powder, Baby Oil, Diapers and Wipes:

• **Avoid powders. We recommend, as do many pediatricians, that you not use powder on your baby at all**. **Drying your baby thoroughly with a soft towel will eliminate the need for powder.** <u>Reason:</u> All powders (even corn starch and mineral-based powders) coat the lungs when inhaled and present a breathing hazard for everyone, but powders are especially harmful to infants. Talc-based powders can be contaminated with asbestos and commercial powders have petrochemical fragrances added.

• **Choose organic aloe vera gel and the botanical oils listed on the previous page instead of baby oil, mineral oil or petroleum jelly.** <u>Reason:</u> Most commercial baby oils contain mineral oil and chemical fragrance; these and petroleum jelly are petrochemicals (petroleum-based) and contain traces of toxic chemicals and metals.

• **Choose cloth diapers or biodegradable disposable diapers.** <u>Reason:</u> When wet, the synthetic chemical absorbents, fragrances and dyes used in standard disposables can cause diaper rash or chemical burns and can pass into the bloodstream.

• **Choose baby wipes without fragrance or synthetic chemicals.** Use page 18 as a guide to safer ingredients. Paper products used on moist skin (toilet paper, tissues and paper towels) should be free from dyes or fragrances and be unbleached.

Kitchen and Foods

1. Safer Cooking/Storage:

a) <u>Conventional Stove</u>: Use glass, ceramic (lead-free), or stainless steel cookware.
<u>Reason</u>: Non-stick coated and aluminum products leach unwanted chemicals or metal into food or air, particularly with high heat or high acid foods. This also applies to plastic and non-stick utensils used for cooking, such as spatulas.

b) <u>Microwave</u>: Use glass or ceramic (lead-free). <u>Reason</u>: Paper products and plastic wrap or bags can leach dioxins (cancer-causing compounds) or other chemicals into your food. Always hand-wash these plastics using warm water with mild dish soap. Research findings are not conclusive with regard to plastics and microwave cooking, so we encourage you to opt for the known safer choices (see next page for more on plastics). In addition, there is debate about the diminished vitamin and nutrient value of food cooked using the microwave. For example, heating breast milk in the microwave has been found to damage beneficial antibodies in the milk.

c) <u>Food packaging and storage</u>: Store in glass or ceramic (lead-free), or stainless steel containers. If you do use plastic wrap or aluminum to seal leftovers, avoid direct contact with food. (For reasons, see **a** and **d**). One safe storage option is to place leftovers in a glass, ceramic, or stainless steel bowl, place a small ceramic or glass plate on top, then seal with plastic wrap or aluminum foil. Avoid purchasing foods in pre-packaged plastic bags that call for boiling/microwaving the food in the bag, in cans with white linings (made from plastic) or in cans with lead-soldered seams (found on some imported canned products). Contact with plastics should be avoided, especially for storage of foods with high oil, fat, and/or acid content.

d) <u>Beverage containers</u>: Use glass or ceramic (lead-free), or stainless steel.
Reason: Plastic, paper, and foam containers have the potential to leach dioxins (carcinogenic compounds) and other chemicals. Leaching increases when these items are used for hot substances, exposed to heat or sunlight, or cleaned using harsh detergents or automatic dish washing. Research on health hazards from plastics, foam and bleached paper products is not conclusive. Some reports show no evidence of health problems. Others indicate links between leached chemicals and hormone/reproductive disorders and even cancer. Since this issue is still being debated, we advise avoiding plastics #3, 6 and 7 (see symbols on next page). You can find the number in the triangle symbol on the bottom of the product; if there is no number assume it is #7. All of these plastics have been found to leach a number of suspect chemicals; the debate is how much is needed to cause harm. **When using plastics, choose safer plastics #1, 2, 4 or 5 whenever possible (see next page); use them as cold beverage containers and hand wash in warm water with mild dish soap.**

SAFER PLASTICS*

AVOID THESE PLASTICS**

Baby Bottles, Nipples, Teethers, and Sippy Cups

The safer choice for baby bottles is tempered glass with silicone nipples. If you decide to use plastic for bottles and sippy cups, choose those made with safer plastics which are currently labeled #5. We list the websites of three companies on page 61 that make baby bottles with safer plastics.* **Do not expose plastics to extreme heat or caustic cleaners. Both have been shown to slowly break down plastics, resulting in the leaching of chemicals.** Hand wash plastic items in warm water with a mild soap, heat formula or milk in glass containers before putting in plastic bottles, and do not use the microwave with any plastic item. For teethers and nipples, silicone is the safer choice compared to rubber or plastic.

* These safer plastics are non-chlorinated and do not contain bisphenol-A (BPA) or phthalates (hormone disrupting chemicals). See pages 39-40 and ewg.org and thegreenguide.com for updates.

** See environmentcalifornia.org/environmental-health under Toxic Baby Bottles for 2007 report.

2. Safer Foods/Beverages:

a) When and how you introduce your baby to foods and beverages other than breast milk should be approved by a qualified health care practitioner. Once these decisions are made, we recommend, whenever possible, choosing foods and beverages with the *USDA Certified Organic* label and/or the *Quality Assurance International-Certified Organic* label. **This labeling guarantees that at least 95% of the ingredients were grown or raised without synthetic fertilizers, synthetic pesticides (herbicides, insecticides, fungicides), antibiotics, growth hormones, bioengineering (e.g., genetically modified organisms [GMOs]), ionizing radiation, or sewage sludge.*** Some studies have also found organic foods to contain more nutrients compared to those conventionally-grown (organic-center.org). The best choice for your health and the environment is to buy local, organically-grown produce and other foods. Most grocery stores now carry some organic produce/products and an increasing consumer demand for these items will increase their availability.

* For more information on label standards for organic foods (including "100% organic" labeling) see: ams.usda.gov/nop. See page 12 for more on the definitions of these labels.

b) Always wash fruits and vegetables, even organic ones, before eating.
<u>Reason</u>: Washing with baking soda or a commercially-available non-toxic fruit and vegetable wash reduces surface traces of **pesticides, fungicides, and wax** on non-organic produce. Washing also safely removes surface dust and dirt that often contains harmful heavy metals such as **lead, cadmium, mercury and other toxins such as flame-retardant chemicals**, which are prevalent in household dust (see page 42). Contaminated dust/dirt is found on both non-organic and organic produce. For information on pesticide content in over 40 conventionally grown fruits and vegetables, see foodnews.org (ewg.org) for best/worst ratings.

c) Avoid seafood consumption for young children and women who are pregnant, breastfeeding or planning to become pregnant. For older children and adults, deep-sea salt-water fish may be safer (with these exceptions: tuna, swordfish, tilefish, Chilean Sea Bass, king mackerel). <u>Reason</u>: Fresh water fish and the exceptions listed above often contain high levels of **mercury**. Also avoid farm-raised fish (unless tested and certified as safe), since studies have revealed high levels of cancer-causing **dioxins and PCBs**. For updates see mercuryaction.org/fish, ewg.org, nrdc.org and seasafe.org.

d) For meat, eggs and milk products, choose organic, cage-free, hormone-free, antibiotic-free, and/or vegetarian-fed. <u>Reason</u>: Consuming products from animals given growth hormones and/or antibiotics can affect human health (e.g., alter the reproductive system and suppress the immune system). In addition, fatty animal products, whether organic or not, tend to contain more industrial toxins such as dioxins and PCBs.

e) Since foods higher on the food chain contain more toxins, consider consuming less animal protein (substituting with vegetable/legume/grain protein) or switching to a vegetarian diet for this and other health/environmental reasons. Consult your health practitioner to ensure adequate daily protein intake. See page 56 for *The Food Revolution* and earthsave.org for more.

f) Use extra-virgin olive (cold-pressed), canola (organic, expeller pressed) or hi-oleic safflower oil. Reason: These are safer oils because they are monounsaturated and more stable than polyunsaturated oils. Polyunsaturated oils break down with heat and digestion to form trans-fatty acids that can contribute to cardiovascular disease. Furthermore, because monounsaturated oils are more stable, they are less likely to become rancid. Rancid oils are carcinogenic (cancer-causing). For olive oil, cold pressed, extra virgin olive oil tends to contain the least chemicals due to minimal processing. For more information on using oils for cooking and baking, as well as safer oils/fats for frying (saturated oils such as coconut, ghee and palm), see spectrumorganics.com and mayoclinic.com.

g) Avoid artificial food additives. Examples of chemical additives to avoid are: monosodium glutamate (MSG), sodium nitrate/nitrite, propylene glycol (PG), polyethylene glycol (PEG), artificial coloring, artificial and questionable preservatives (e.g., BHT/BHA, sodium benzoate, potassium benzoate), artificial flavors, and artificial sweeteners. See page 15 for more.

h) Choose safer sugars and sugar substitutes. Avoid artificial sweeteners such as aspartame, sucralose, acesulfame-k and others under trademarked names. Safe and more nutritious choices include unrefined/unprocessed cane sugar, rice syrup, barley malt, agave syrup, and fruit juices. Honey is another good choice. However **never use honey for canning or preserving** because of the potential growth of botulinus toxin (causes botulism) and **never give honey to babies under 1 year of age** as they are unable to handle even the trace amounts of this toxin found in natural honey. If in doubt about a sweetener, do a web search to review reported or suspected health issues. Be especially cautious with products labeled "sugar-free", "reduced-sugar" or even "low-carb", as these are likely to contain artificial, chemical sweeteners.

i) Choose foods, preferably less processed ones, that are not artificially or otherwise altered. For example, a whole grain product made with unbleached whole wheat flour is a better choice than one made with white "enriched" flour. Reason: Less processed foods typically have a greater vitamin, mineral and fiber content and are less likely to contain artificial colors/flavors/sweeteners or chemical preservatives. **Read ingredient lists carefully** as package labels can be misleading: we have found whole wheat products containing sucralose with no indication on the front of the package that this artificial sweetener was added. Further, claims of "natural flavoring", "natural ingredients", "reduced sugar" and "sugar-free" do not mean that it is wholesome and safe.

j) For water used for cooking or drinking, consider a filtration system.

Tap water concerns: Chloroform, a common pollutant found in drinking water, is formed when chlorine (added as a disinfectant) combines with organic matter found naturally in water. Chloroform is a suspected carcinogen and can cause liver and kidney damage. Metal pipes can leach pollutants including **lead, cadmium, copper, iron, and zinc** into drinking water. **PVC pipes, tubing, and even vinyl garden hoses** leach toxins such as lead and the endocrine-disrupting chemicals bisphenol-A and phthalates into water, especially when water is hot. Other pollutants found in tap water include **pesticides and industrial chemicals**. Water treatment facilities are designed mainly to disinfect water (kill bacteria) and not to purify it (remove chemical contaminants). **Installing a water filter or filtration system for purification requires some effort and cost, but given the health benefits, it is well worth it.** Options include reverse osmosis, activated carbon filters, and distillers. A review of these is beyond the scope of this book, but there are many sources available to help you choose. See epa.gov/safewater and nsf.org (under Consumer) for more information. See page 11 for health risks of fluoridated water.

Bottled water is an alternative to filtration but disadvantages include poor reliability, (quality/purity varies widely) and the lack of industry/government standards. For safer plastic containers see pages 21-22 or use stainless steel. Reviews on bottled water can be found in *Consumer Reports* and are available online. Disadvantages of bottled water include cost, bacteria in re-used bottles, and the environmental impact of container disposal.

Safer water for bathing and showering: For municipal water, consider adding filters to bath faucets and shower heads to remove chlorine, chloroform, and contaminants such as lead. **For well water,** in addition to water filtration, make sure pipes are lead-free and test (generally once a year) for bacteria, nitrates and other environmental pollutants you suspect.

Cleaning Products

Our great-grandparents used safe, inexpensive, natural ingredients like vinegar and baking soda to disinfect and deodorize. Today, most Americans use a variety of expensive, toxic chemicals to do the same jobs. **The majority of American homes contain several gallons of toxic substances, most in the form of cleaning products.**

As some of the most dangerous items in the home, cleaning products are regulated by the Consumer Product Safety Commission under the Federal Hazardous Substances Act (FHSA). The FHSA states that if a product can cause substantial personal injury or illness, it must carry a Warning, Caution or Danger label. This labeling is required on any product containing chemicals that are toxic, flammable, corrosive, radioactive, combustible under pressure, or act as irritants or strong sensitizers. The FHSA is concerned with short-term or acute effects (e.g., burning eyes, sneezing, headache, skin rashes), not the effects of chronic exposure. **Chronic, long-term effects are not required to be listed on a product's label. Potential effects from prolonged exposure to the toxic fumes of cleaning products include: respiratory problems, cancer, heart disease, immune system impairment, and birth defects.**

You can clean your home just as effectively without using chemicals that create toxic fumes harmful to your family. In most cases, **natural substances are less expensive,** and despite what many manufacturers would have you believe, you don't need a different product for each cleaning need in your home.

<u>Most household cleaning can be done with one or more of these</u>

- 50/50 solution of vinegar and water (disinfects, removes stains and odors)[*]
- baking soda (removes stains, neutralizes odors)
- liquid castile soap (for general cleaning, dishes; dilute for hand soap)
- lemon juice (cuts grease)
- non-chlorine scouring powder (e.g., Bon Ami®, made with a naturally occurring mineral)
- microfiber cleaning cloths (use wet with any of the above for cleaning or dry for dusting)

<u>Additional cleaners for specific jobs</u>[**]

- borax (disinfects, neutralizes odors, laundry booster)
- washing soda (removes stains, cuts grease, neutralizes odors; use carefully on fabric)
- sodium percarbonate powder (a chlorine-free, mineral-based bleach substitute)
- natural enzyme-based (bio-cleaner) stain removers

[*] We recommend using organic white distilled vinegar, not vinegar made with synthetic acetic acid. Use gloves and good ventilation.

[**] Use gloves when working with these items. Although they are safer options, they can be harsh on skin.

Recipe for a Safer All-Purpose Cleaner

½ teaspoon liquid castile soap made from natural plant oils
2 teaspoons borax or baking soda
1 teaspoon vinegar or lemon juice
2 cups hot water

Combine ingredients in a spray bottle and shake.*
For heavy cleaning, add ½ teaspoon washing soda (and wear gloves).

For a disinfectant effect and a natural fragrance, add several drops of one of these antiseptic, pure essential oils: lavender, tea tree, rosemary, orange blossom, or eucalyptus.**

*Use caution with any spray, especially in the nursery, since aromatic sprays can irritate the eyes, nose, and/or lungs. See note on page 29 for type of vinegar.
**Although pure essential oils are natural, anyone (especially babies) may be sensitive or allergic to them. For safest use, do a final rinse of surfaces with plain water and a clean cloth.

Safer Drain Cleaner/Declogger

Pour ½ cup baking soda and 1 cup hot cider or organic white vinegar (can heat in microwave) into drain and let sit for 15 minutes. Flush with very hot water. Note: if using synthetic distilled vinegar, do not heat first because airborne fumes may contain contaminants.

Special Note on Cleaning the Nursery:

Baking soda, vinegar, and castile soap are the safest and most effective ways to keep the nursery clean. Baking soda will clean and neutralize odors. Vinegar is a natural disinfectant; it safely and effectively prevents the growth of bacteria. Castile soap is a safe, effective cleanser. If you choose castile soap with tea tree oil added, you'll get the natural antiseptic and anti-fungal properties of tea tree as well. Lavender is another good essential oil that can be added to castile soap for its antiseptic properties. However, your baby might be sensitive to the odor of these essential oils so use while your baby is not in the room and air the room out. Always finish cleaning by rinsing thoroughly with plain water any cleaned surface with which your baby will have direct contact.

Ideally, all new clothing, sheets, bumpers, blankets, stuffed animals and fabric decorations should be washed several times before use in order to remove chemicals from the fabric (see page 42).

Additional Tips for Non-toxic Cleaning:

- **Choose the least toxic option.** For example, using a doormat and removing shoes reduces tracking pollutants indoors and the need to wash floors or shampoo carpets frequently.

- **Less is usually safer.** For cleaning products, especially those with harsh chemicals, unless product directions state otherwise, try a lesser amount first to see if it will do the job.

- **Avoid the use of ammonia or bleach because of hazardous fumes. If you do choose to use these, never mix the ammonia with the bleach (or vinegar)**; these combinations produce toxic, potentially-fatal fumes.

- **Avoid products that come in aerosol spray cans.** The spray sends a mist of chemicals into the air, where it is inhaled or lands on the skin or eyes.

- **Washing soda is composed of naturally occurring minerals and is good for scouring hard surfaces.** It's moderately caustic, so you need to wear gloves. Leave it on overnight as an oven cleaner to allow the minerals to do their job. Use sparingly on fabric, as it can weaken fibers and remove dyes.

- **Don't store chemicals under the kitchen or bathroom sinks where children may have access.** Keep chemicals in the garage or another area away from children and pets.

- **For safer clothes-whitening products, look for bleach alternatives** with hydrogen peroxide or percarbonate powder. Strong sunlight can also effectively lighten clothes.

Buying Safer Cleaning/Household Products

There are many safer, effective products available for purchase in retail and online stores that sell natural products. These range from safer glass cleaners and automatic dish washing powders/liquids to safer adhesives and paints. We list companies that sell safer household products as well as information on how to find non-toxic cleaners and recipes in *How to Learn More*.

When buying household products, look for safer ingredients (page 29) and the following terms on the product label or ingredients list:

- biodegradable
- enzyme-based (stain removers)
- non-toxic (see page 35)
- chlorine-free
- phosphate-free (liquid laundry detergents)
- non-petroleum based surfactants (in all-purpose cleaners)
- VOC-free or low-VOC (in paints, markers, refinishing products, glues)
- natural fragrance (from essential oils)

COMMON INGREDIENTS TO AVOID

Ingredient (most are VOCs)	Commonly used as/in
acetone	stain/nail polish removers, permanent markers
antibacterial (triclosan)	soaps, antibacterial cleaners, clothing, toys, sneakers
ammonia	glass/all-purpose cleaners, antibacterial soap
fragrances (artificial)	cleaning and personal care products (see page 13)
benzene	solvents, paints, fragrances, cosmetics
bleach/chlorine	laundry products, scouring powder
cresol	air fresheners, floor/furniture polish, perm. markers
dyes	dishwashing liquid, laundry detergent
formaldehyde/formalin (see page 15)	disinfectants, air fresheners, permanent markers / hair spray, nail polish, mouthwash, epoxy
lead	ceramic glazes, hair color, older paint
lye (sodium hydroxide)	drain and oven cleaners
naphthalene	air fresheners, permanent markers, moth balls
paradichlorobenzene	air fresheners, moth balls
perchloroethylene (PERC)	rug shampoo, dry cleaning
petroleum distillates	floor/furniture polishes, metal cleaners
phenol	floor/furniture polish, disinfectants, nail polish
sodium hypochlorite	bleach, disinfectants, mold/mildew cleaners
tetrachloroethylene	dry cleaning
toluene	nail polish, permanent markers
xylene	paint, air fresheners, nail polish

Since manufacturers of cleaning products are not required by law to provide a complete list ingredients, here are two ways to determine whether or not a product is safe.

1) If the terms **Poison**, **Danger**, **Warning**, or **Caution** are anywhere on the label, you can be sure the product contains harmful ingredients.

2) Look for companies/manufacturers who provide a **complete list of natural ingredients** on the product label. Some manufacturers claim their products are **non-toxic** or **environmentally safe**, but since these terms are not legally defined, the only way to know for sure whether a product is safe is to read and evaluate a complete list of both active and inactive (inert) ingredients.

Around the Home

1. Air Quality

Every item in your home, from your baby's crib to new carpeting, and the products used to clean these items, can directly affect air quality. Household chemicals, cigarette/cigar smoke, mold/mildew, and fumes from "out-gassing" of VOCs in home furnishings all decrease air quality. **According to the EPA, indoor air is likely to be 7 to 100 times more contaminated than outdoor air. The first step to improving indoor air quality is to locate and remove the sources of the problem.** For example, new furnishings for the nursery may require "airing" out before use (see page 7).

The next best way to improve air quality is with good ventilation and the easiest way to ventilate a room is to open a window. A window opened just one inch (even for short periods of time) can make a big difference in indoor air quality.

In addition to improved ventilation with outdoor air or an exhaust fan, air cleaners (with approved HEPA filters) and air conditioners (with clean filters) decrease airborne pollutants and greatly improve air quality. These are better options than opening a window if the outdoor air is contaminated (e.g., vehicle exhaust or pollution from local manufacturing/power plants). Be sure to change or clean filters in air conditioners, air purifiers, heating units, and vacuum bags/filters according to manufacturers' instructions.

2. Carpeting

Standard commercial carpets, the adhesive used for installation, and chemicals applied to the carpet fiber to improve stain-resistance emit VOCs, including formaldehyde, toluene and benzene. Many of these chemicals have been found in the blood and urine of healthy children and adults, adding to their chemical body burden. These chemicals can cause cancer and other health problems including damage to both the immune and nervous systems. **Acute symptoms of VOC exposure may include:** headache, eye/nose/throat irritation, shortness of breath, fatigue, wheezing, asthma, migraines, seizures, flu-like symptoms, impaired memory or an inability to concentrate.*

Infants and young children (and pets!) are at increased risk for these health problems because they sit and lie on carpets while playing and napping. As explained earlier, because children's nervous systems are still developing, they are more vulnerable to toxins than are adults. In addition to chemicals in the carpeting, dirt, mold, bacteria and other contaminants listed below are more likely to get trapped in carpet fibers making it difficult to clean thoroughly.

Recommendations for safer carpet and flooring choices are listed on the next page. Regardless of the type of floor covering you choose, removing shoes when coming indoors can significantly reduce contaminants such as mercury, lead, bacteria, pesticides, herbicides, and arsenic, which are commonly tracked inside. It has been estimated that removing shoes alone can reduce the amount of lead brought into a home by 70%.

*epa.gov/iaq/pubs   bchealthguide.org   ehponline.org   http://database.healthandenvironment.org

Safer Carpet and Flooring Choices

- Choose natural fiber carpeting (such as organic cotton, wool, jute or hemp) that hasn't had chemical treatments including dyes, stain protection, flame-resistance, or pesticides (e.g., insecticides, moth-proofing, and mildew-cides).*

- Choose adhesives made from natural plant materials such as plant terpin, citrus oils, herbal extracts or beeswax. Tack carpets in place rather than gluing them down.

- If you choose standard commercial carpeting, air out the room for a minimum of 2 weeks after installation or until VOC fumes have dissipated. Using an air purifier that removes VOCs or Zeolite (in bag or pouch) are safe options to help reduce VOC fumes.

- As a safer alternative to carpeting, install hard wood floors or ceramic tile and use washable area rugs where needed.

- Choose area rugs made of natural fibers since they eliminate the need for toxic adhesives and can be cleaned more thoroughly than wall-to-wall carpeting.

- For safer carpet cleaning, use non-toxic cleaners (unscented or scented with natural essential oils; see **Cleaning Products**). Freshen carpets by sprinkling baking soda generously, leave for 20 minutes, and vacuum. Zeolite is also a safe option to reduce odors from carpets. Avoid commercial carpet "fresheners" that simply cover up odors with chemical/synthetic fragrances.

  * See home-expo.com and use the search option for safer carpeting/flooring and home furnishing choices. Other sources for safer home furnishings and building materials: greensage.com, healthyhome.com, thegreenguide.com, organicgrace.com, greendepot.com

3. Plastic Toys, Furniture and Home Furnishings

Plastics contain chemicals that are likely to leach out with exposure to heat, harsh cleaners, and when exposed to moisture as when a child sucks or chews on the product. Chemicals and toxic heavy metals (such as lead) found in some plastics are linked to serious health problems such as cancer, hormone/reproductive disorders, and impaired brain development. Recent research suggests that even at low levels these toxins may be harmful. Decades of "safety" studies reported by the plastics industry have not addressed these effects on child development.

We recommend avoiding plastics containing polyvinyl chloride (PVC) or polystyrene (PS), known as #3 and #6 plastics respectively, polycarbonate (PC) plastics (#7 plastic). These plastics are widely used in many products and pose a health risk.* We advise not exposing plastic items to heat or caustic cleaners; both can cause leaching of chemicals. These questionable plastics are found in many squeeze toys, teethers, pacifiers, rattles, bath toys, playpens, cribs, high chairs, sippy cups, baby bottles, baby bibs, shower curtains, garden hoses, plastic pools, etc.

* See environmentcalifornia.org/environmental-health, ewg.org, healthychild.org and besafenet.com for updates on plastics and health.

Safer Toys and Furniture

Safer plastics for toys, furniture, and other household items include polyethylene (#1, #2 and #4) and polypropylene (#5). These plastics require the use of less toxic additives, for example, they are non-chlorinated, phthalate-free, PVC-free and BPA-free. Safer choices are silicone or plastics currently numbered:

As with other plastics, we advise hand washing with mild soap and not exposing them to harsh cleaners, strong sunlight, or heat (e.g., do not put in the dishwasher or leave in a hot vehicle).

Toys made of organic, natural fibers are safer alternatives for children of any age and especially important for babies. Look for dolls and stuffed animals made from organic cotton, hemp or wool. Otherwise, choose stuffed toys that can first be washed to reduce toxins such as flame-retardants, residual pesticides, fragrances, and antibacterials. Avoid toys, bibs, furniture (e.g., high chairs) and other items that contain or are treated with antibacterial chemicals. On page 63, we list companies that sell safer, non-toxic stuffed animals and toys.

Unpainted wooden toys are safer choices. <u>Reason:</u> Painted toys may contain lead, mercury and/or other toxins. Safety is a concern for new toys, those with old/antique painted wood/plastic/metal, and those with flaking paint. Since the term "non-toxic" is not regulated by the government, buying toys or other products solely on that basis does not guarantee they are free from harmful substances (phthalates, PVC, BPA, lead, etc.). Due to recent safety issues, we advise checking online at cpsc.gov (Consumer Product Safety Commission), recalls.gov and healthytoys.org for recalls and safety testing of toys. We note that most recalled items have been manufactured for US companies in countries outside of the US, Canada, and Europe.

Choose playground sets *not* made from pressure-treated wood. Playgrounds and decks already built with pressure-treated wood should be sealed regularly with an approved sealant to ensure that toxins such as arsenic do not leach out.

4. Baby's Clothing, Bedding and Mattress

In order to remove chemicals and dust, all new clothing and bedding should be washed several times. Choosing **organic materials** (e.g., organic cotton, hemp or wool) will guarantee that pesticides and other toxic chemicals were not used in production.* **We strongly recommend avoiding dryer sheets, laundry detergents and fabric softeners with chemical fragrances (see page 13), as well as any clothing, bibs, shoes or fabric treated with antibacterial chemicals**.

Flame-retardant chemicals applied in the manufacturing process are a concern in baby's clothing, blankets, etc. These chemicals are a common component of household dust and have been found in human body tissues (including breast milk) around the world. Flame-retardants are potential carcinogens and the long-term effects of accumulation in the body are still unknown. 100% wool mattresses are naturally flame-retardant and meet governmental standards for flame retardance without added chemicals.

Most dry cleaning uses toxic solvents, such as perchloroethylene (PERC or PCE). Inhaling these fumes can cause acute symptoms such as dizziness, nausea, fatigue and long term exposure can cause liver damage. The good news is that most items marked "dry clean only" can safely be washed; you just need to learn how (see *Better Basics for the Home* on page 55). If you choose to dry clean, use "green" businesses that do not use PERC. Remove items from packaging and hang in well-ventilated area (preferably outside) before use.

* We list several of the many websites that sell organic bedding, mattresses, clothing etc. on page 61.

5. Household Decor

Avoid burning paraffin or petroleum-based wax candles. In addition to the petroleum and benzene in these candles, the wicks are often made with plastic, lead, or other metals that release toxins into the air when burned. **100% beeswax, soy, or plant-wax candles that are unscented (or scented only with pure essential oils) and have cotton wicks are safer options.**

Store-bought flowers may be beautiful, but unless they are wildcrafted or organically grown, they're likely to have been heavily sprayed with pesticides (see page 45). For safer floral choices, look for USDA Organic, Wildcrafted and/or Veriflora-labeled flowers and plants. One web store that meets these standards is organicbouquet.com.

Some indoor plants naturally reduce common indoor air pollutants such as formaldehyde, benzene, and trichloroethylene. Examples of plants that remove airborne toxins include: spider plant, palm, fern, ficus (such as rubber and fig varieties), Gerbera daisy, and chrysanthemum (see *How to Grow Fresh Air* on page 56). Most allergists do not recommend placing live plants in bedrooms because of airborne mold spores from potting soil. This is especially true of plants that require frequent watering.

6. Paint and Wallpaper

Homes built prior to 1978 should be tested for lead contamination, especially if peeling paint is present on any surfaces inside or outside. Your pediatrician should also be notified so that your child's blood lead levels can be monitored. If lead is a problem, contact your local or state public health office to obtain safe procedures for lead abatement/removal. Do not start a renovation project or sand surfaces with old paint before ruling out a lead paint issue.*

If you have to paint, wallpaper, or refinish furniture or floors before baby's arrival, do it as early as possible. An EPA study found that after painting, VOC levels indoors were 1000 times greater than outdoors. Give painted areas several weeks (or even months) to air out, keeping windows open whenever possible. **Use water-based paint with "zero" or low-VOC content** (afmsafecoat.com, alerg.com, ecosorganicpaints.com, safepaint.net, ecosafetyproducts.com). Look for paints with low levels of fungicides and biocides (added to prevent mildew and increase shelf-life) that have natural rather than chemical pigments. Natural and milk-based paints (realmilkpaint.com, greenplanetpaints.com, bioshieldpaint.com) are very low in VOCs and do not contain biocides.

Use adequate ventilation to remove any detectable odors from "out-gassing" before anyone (including pets) is exposed to a room (or furniture) with freshly painted or wallpapered surfaces. This is especially important for pregnant women, babies and young children.

* For more information on lead paint see: epa.gov/lead   www.hud.gov/offices/lead   clearcorps.org

7. Pest, Weed and Flea/Tick Control*

It is estimated that homeowners and lawn care companies use over 600 million pounds of pesticides annually in the United States. A pesticide is defined by law as any substance intended to prevent, repel, destroy or control any pest. **Put simply, pesticides are poisons.** Pesticides include insecticides, herbicides, fungicides, antimicrobials, and chemicals that kill rodents.

Most people falsely assume that pesticides are safe for home and commercial use because these products are so readily available in stores. People also falsely assume that an EPA registration number on a product is an indication of safety, when in fact EPA registration is required for a pesticide because it is an immediate safety hazard. When used or tracked inside the home, pesticides can remain on rugs, toys and furniture for months and even years, allowing for continued exposure. Since pesticides persist and accumulate in body tissues, they pose long-term health threats.

* Sources: pesticide.org   beyondpesticides.org   healthychild.org   loe.org   ehponline.org
ABCs of Toxicology, Basic Definitions. M. Kemple. *Journal of Pesticide Reform* 21(4), 2001.

What makes these chemicals unsafe for children, adults, and pets?

Many of the synthetic ingredients in pesticides are derived from the same chemicals that were designed to kill humans in chemical warfare. The difference is that commercial products sold as pesticides are diluted and minimally altered, often with artificial fragrances added. In addition, most contain substances labeled as "inert", yet these so-called inert substances can also pose serious health risks.

Medical records and research findings show that the majority of leukemia, brain tumors and other cancers in children are linked to pesticides. In addition, evidence from human case studies point to these toxins as suspected causes of childhood disorders such as mental retardation, learning disabilities, autism, asthma, anxiety, depression and attention disorders.* Not only are most pesticides hazardous to the health of people at any age, they also damage the environment, harm pets and wildlife, and contaminate drinking water.

* Sources: Pesticides and Childhood Cancer. S. H. Zahm & M. H. Ward. *Environmental Health Perspectives* 106 (3), 1998.
  In Harm's Way: Toxic Threats to Child Development. Greater Boston Physicians for Social Responsibility, 2000. (psr.igc.org)
  Pesticide Literature Review: Systematic Review of Pesticide Human Health Effects. The Ontario College of Family Physicians, 2004. (ocfp.on.ca)

pesticide.org	healthandenvironment.org	mindfully.org	beyondpesticides.org
healthychild.org	childenvironment.org	chem-tox.com/pesticides	loe.org

TO PUT THIS IN A POSITIVE LIGHT:

If we had to choose one area that would have the biggest impact on the health of children, it would be this one. Using safer options for pest control can help to ensure the safety and well-being of our children and our environment, now and for future generations. We can do this by choosing safe (non-toxic) and minimal risk (least toxic) solutions for pest control.

On the following pages, we list examples of these safer solutions as well as resources for finding more information on this important topic.

Safe, Non-toxic Options for Pest Control

Identifying and removing the sources (causes) of the pest problem is the first and most important step to eliminating it. These are sources of food, water or shelter for pests found inside or outside the home. Some measures to control and prevent pests:

- **Keep your home, especially the kitchen, dry and clean (free of crumbs, dirty dishes, clutter, dampness and standing water) in order to prevent pests.** Use window and door screens and seal/caulk cracks in foundations, doors, and walls to prevent pests from entering the home.

- **For general indoor insect control:** Trim bushes, plants and trees back from touching the outside surfaces of the house, windows, steps and foundation. This helps prevent insects from entering the home.

- **To help prevent termite infestation**: Remove wood debris from yard and foundation area and be sure that unsealed wood is not in contact with the ground. Woodpiles should be kept at least 10-15 feet away from the home, garage or shed.

- **For roach and rodent control**: Store snacks, cereals, baking supplies, pet food, etc. in sealed containers. Remove or relocate bird feeders away from the home to reduce a likely source of food for rodents.

- **For mosquito control:** Remove outside containers and debris that collect water. Mosquitoes lay their eggs in standing water.

- **For control of insects in the lawn and garden:** Raise beneficial insects that eat detrimental bugs. For example, ladybugs eat aphids, nematodes (tiny worms) feed on insect larvae and praying mantises eat many pests in gardens and trees.

Safe, Non-toxic Weed Control

For spot weed control: Apply full-strength vinegar directly onto weeds.

For lawn weed control: Certain weeds indicate specific conditions or deficiencies of the soil; correcting these soil conditions and seeding with weed-resistant grass species will help to prevent weeds. Annual weeds can be controlled with non-toxic, enzyme-based pre-emergents such as corn gluten.

Minimal Risk (least toxic) Pest Control Options

- Use food grade diatomaceous earth (DE) with less than 1% free silica (pool-grade DE is not recommended). Sprinkle DE (avoid inhalation) or use as wettable powder inside or outside your home at entry points for pests. You can also use equal parts of dry DE and boric acid. Boric acid or borax alone can be used for surface application to kill pests with minimal risk to people. NOTE: Using boric acid or borax requires caution in areas that are accessible to children or pets. These agents do not give off toxic fumes, but are not safe if powder is accidentally consumed, inhaled or comes in contact with skin.

- Properly maintained bait traps are safer options as they have low or no volatility (i.e., not readily changing to vapor). Risk remains for accidental skin contact or consumption.

More information on non-toxic and minimal risk pest control solutions can be found on the websites listed on pages 60 and 64. The following books provide a wealth of information including simple recipes to make your own safe, effective, insect repellents and yard control solutions for insects including ticks and mosquitoes.

> *Better Basics for the Home: Simple Solutions for Less Toxic Living,* by Annie Berthold-Bond. Rodale, 2005, 2nd edition.

> *The Bug Stops Here,* by Steve Tvedten. Free online at: thebestcontrol.com

> *Home Safe Home,* by Debra Lynn Dadd. Tarcher, 1997.

How to Identify Minimal Risk Pest Control Products:

- **Look for the term "Poison-Free" on the label.** This does not guarantee a product is safe, but is a good indication of less harmful ingredients.

- **Look for products *without* an EPA Pesticide Registration number.*** If it's on the product it is usually in small print, so read the label carefully. When pest control products are approved for sale in the U.S. *without* an EPA registration, this means the product was rated as "minimal risk". These products are then exempt from EPA registration and should have the "minimal risk" label as defined on the following page.

* NOTE: Some low risk pest control products do have an EPA registration number. For example, milky spore is biologically harmless to people, pets and wildlife, yet an effective method to kill grubs. The risk to people is from particle inhalation of powder during application. To help discern risk, read the required EPA cautionary statements and product application instructions. In addition, a search on the product's ingredients (use the websites on pages 52, 58 and 60) will help you evaluate the potential for harm to people, pets and/or the environment.

- **Look for products with the following on the label:**

  Minimal Risk Product EPA exempted under FIFRA Section 25(b)*

  This labeling means that the product does not qualify for the EPA's definition of a pesticide that needs registration. Products with this minimal risk label do not pose an immediate toxic hazard and are less likely to have chronic or low-level effects than products with an EPA registration. These products will still have precautionary statements that should be heeded.

  * Federal Insecticide, Fungicide and Rodenticide Act, 1947

- **If you decide to hire a professional to take care of a pest problem, look for a company that uses Integrated Pest Management (IPM).** IPM professionals are trained to use prevention and least-toxic methods of pest control. Go to beyondpesticides.org and click on "Info Services" and then "Safety Source For Pest Management" to locate an IPM company near you. For more information on IPM see: http://www.epa.gov/pesticides/factsheets/ipm.htm

For more information on pesticides and pest control:

The following web resources include up-to-date reports on the commercially available pesticides you may now be using as well as non-toxic alternatives. We note that many commercial lawn and pest control companies claim (or imply with ads showing children and pets around the product) that their EPA-registered pesticides do not pose health risks and are safe for children and pets; however, the EPA prohibits by law such claims for registered pesticides. **When you look up the ingredients (both active and inert) in most commercially available pesticides, you will see why safety claims should not be made.**

pesticide.org
pesticides.org
epa.gov/pesticides
lesstoxicguide.ca
beyondpesticides.org
healthychild.org
ewg.org
ehponline.org

V. *Coping with Chemical Exposure*

Everyone in today's world is exposed to chemicals and, thus, has a chemical body burden. Recent research has found detectable levels of many synthetic chemicals in the body fluids and tissues of healthy children and adults. Other research has linked at least 180 human health conditions with exposure to environmental toxins, yet there is no way to predict who may be harmed, how much is too much, or what acute/chronic health problems may result. Thus, we have advocated that it's worthwhile, wherever possible, to reduce exposure to known and suspected toxins.

We are particularly concerned with exposure for babies and young children, but research shows that we are all at risk. Furthermore, certain individuals are more reactive or sensitive to a chemical(s) due to prior exposure to other toxins, prior illness, and/or individual differences in the ability to detoxify (e.g., innate liver/cell enzyme differences). A person with heightened reactions to chemicals may also have increased reactions to a wide range of environmental substances (e.g., dust, mold, pollen, dander) and/or various foods (e.g., food allergy, gluten-intolerance). While it is not clear which physiological mechanisms are responsible for increases in sensitivity, measures to improve overall immune system functioning can be helpful in reducing the negative effects of exposure to chemicals. Identifying and reducing toxic exposure is a prudent first step, but other important measures can benefit anyone's immune system. For example, good nutrition, vitamin/herbal/mineral supplementation to improve detoxification, identifying and avoiding allergens, regular exercise, and stress/anxiety reduction can all improve immune system functioning.

We recommend seeking help from trained medical professionals who can: identify health problems resulting from toxic exposure, provide ways to reduce further exposure, and recommend an overall program to strengthen the immune system. We list resources below on health and the immune system as well as websites that will help keep you up-to-date on this rapidly growing area of study in medicine and psychology.

Suggested reading on improving immune system functioning:

Boost Your Child's Immune System: A Program and Recipes for Raising Strong, Healthy Kids by Lucy Burney. Newmarket Press, 2005.

Boosting Immunity: Creating Wellness Naturally by Len Saputo and Nancy Faass, Eds. New World Library, 2002.

Dr. Braly's Food Allergy & Nutrition Revolution by James Braly and Laura Torbet. McGraw Hill, 1998.

Encyclopedia of Natural Medicine by Michael Murrey and Joseph Pizzorno. Bookmart Ltd., 1999.

Prescription for Nutritional Healing by Phyllis A. Balch. Avery Press, 2006.

Superimmunity for Kids: What to Feed Your Children to Keep Them Healthy Now, and Prevent Disease in Their Future by Leo Galland and Dian Dincin Buchman. Dell, 1989.

Your Health, Your Choice: Your Complete Personal Guide to Wellness, Nutrition & Disease Prevention by M. Ted Morter, Jr. Fell Publishers, 1995.

Websites with updates/newsletters:

environmentalhealthnews.org

drgreene.com (see Environmental Health)

featuresblogs.chicagotribune.com/features_julieshealthclub

healthandenvironment.org

ehponline.org

lef.org

VI. *How to Learn More*

REFERENCES AND RESOURCES

Baking Soda, Over 500 Fabulous, Fun and Frugal Uses You've Probably Never Thought Of by Vicki Lansky. Book Peddlers, 2004, 2nd Edition.

Better Basics for the Home: Simple Solutions for Less Toxic Living by Annie Berthold-Bond. Rodale, 2005, 2nd Edition.

Chemical Exposures: Low Levels and High Stakes by Nicholas A. Ashford and Claudia S. Miller. Wiley, 1998, 2nd Edition.

Clean House, Clean Planet: Clean Your House for Pennies a Day the Safe, Non-toxic Way by Karen Logan. Simon & Schuster, 1997.

Creating a Healthy Household: The Ultimate Guide for Healthier, Safer, Less-Toxic Living by Lynn Marie Bower. Healthy Home Institute, 2000.

Drop-Dead Gorgeous: Protecting Yourself from the Hidden Dangers of Cosmetics by Kim Erickson. McGraw-Hill, 2002.

Dying to Look Good by Christina Hoza Farlow. KISS for Health Publishing, 2005.

Environmental Toxicants and Developmental Disabilities by Susan M. Koger, Ted Schettler and Bernard Weiss. *American Psychologist* 60 (3) 243-255, 2005.

Excitotoxins: The Taste that Kills by Russell L. Blaylock. Health Press, 1997.

The Food Revolution: How Your Diet Can Help Save Your Life and the World by John Robbins. Conari Press, 2001.

Green This! Volume 1: Greening Your Cleaning by Deirdre Imus. Simon & Schuster, 2007.

Healthy Baby Toxic World: Practical Ways to Protect Your Baby During Pregnancy and Infancy by Melody Milam Potter and Erin E. Milam. New Harbinger Publications, 1999.

Healthy Living in a Toxic World: Simple Ways to Protect Yourself and Your Family from Hidden Health Risks by Cynthia E. Fincher. Pinon Press, 1996.

Home Safe Home: Protecting Yourself and Your Family from Everyday Toxins and Harmful Household Products by Debra Lynn Dadd. Tarcher, 1997.

How to Grow Fresh Air: 50 Houseplants that Purify Your Home or Office by BC Wolverton. Penguin Books, 1999, 2nd Printing.

The Hundred Year Lie: How Food and Medicine are Destroying Your Health by Randall Fitzgerald. Dutton, 2006.

In Harm's Way: Toxic Threats to Child Development, A report by Greater Boston Physicians for Social Responsibility, 2000. Get a copy at 617-497-7440 or free download at psr.igc.org

Mothers and Others for a Livable Planet Guide to Natural Baby Care: Non-Toxic and Environmentally Friendly Ways to Take Care of Your New Child by Mindy Pennybacker and Aisha Ikramuddin. Wiley,1999.

The Naturally Clean Home: 101 Safe and Easy Herbal Formulas for Nontoxic Cleansers by Karyn Siegal-Maier. Storey Books, 1999.

The Newman's Own® Organics Guide to a Good Life: Simple Measures that Benefit You and the Place You Live by Nell Newman with Joseph D'Agnese. Random House, 2003.

Not Just a Pretty Face: The Ugly Side of the Beauty Industry by Stacey Malkan. New Society Publishers, 2007.

Our Stolen Future: Are We Threatening Our Fertility, Intelligence, and Survival?—A Scientific Detective Story by Theo Colburn, Dianne Dumanski and John Peterson Myers. Plume/Penguin, 1996.

Our Toxic World: A Wake Up Call by Doris Rapp. Environmental Medical Research, 2004.

Pesticide Literature Review: Systematic Review of Pesticide Human Health Effects by The Ontario College of Family Physicians, 2004. (ocfp.on.ca)

Raising Baby Green: The Earth Friendly Guide to Pregnancy, Childbirth, and Baby Care by Alan Greene, Jeanette Pavini, and Teresa Foy DiGeronimo. Jossey-Bass, 2007.

Raising Healthy Children in a Toxic World by Philip Landrigan, Herbert Needleman and Mary Landrigan. Rodale, 2001.

The Right Start: The Need to Eliminate Toxic Chemicals from Baby Products, USPIRG Education Fund, October, 2005. Free download at: http://safefromtoxics.org/reports/therightstart.pdf

Safe Shopper's Bible: A Consumer's Guide to Non-Toxic Household Products, Cosmetics, and Food by David Steinman and Samuel S. Epstein. Wiley, 1995.

Silent Scourge: Children, Pollution, and Why Scientists Disagree by Colleen Moore. Oxford University Press, 2002.

Staying Well in a Toxic World by Lynn Lawson. Lynnwood Press, 2000.

What's in Your Food? The Truth About Food Additives from Aspartame to Xanthum Gum by Bill Statham. Running Press Book Publishers, 2007.

The following are some of the many websites that provide information on nontoxic living. These include sites with resource links as well as sites that sell safer products. We start with a list of websites that have search options using a keyword such as an ingredient, chemical name or health/safety issue. We advise checking and comparing several sources when doing a search. When purchasing products, check the ingredients list, read product information carefully, and/or call the company if you need more information on product safety and ingredients.

websites with SEARCH OPTIONS

healthychild.org	Healthy Child, Healthy World
sis.nlm.nih.gov	National Library of Medicine's site with extensive search options
scorecard.org	Safety ratings of chemicals found in household products
hazard.com/msds	Safety rating/information; Search by chemical name
epa.gov/chemfact	EPA Chemical Fact Sheet; Information may be outdated
aubrey-organics.com	Dictionary of natural ingredients;10 synthetic chemicals to avoid
ourstolenfuture.org	Scientific updates on toxins
nrdc.org/health	Natural Resources Defense Council; Site search on toxins
atsdr.cdc.gov/cxcx3.html	Toxicology Profiles; Top 20 hazardous substances; Site search
inchem.org	Safety of chemicals in personal care, food & household products
cspinet.org	Center for Science in the Public Interest
ewg.org	Environmental Working Group (Quick Index)
loe.org	Public Radio's Living on Earth
newstarget.com	Independent news source on health and environment
cosmeticsdatabase.com	Environmental Working Group's product/ingredient safety database
turi.org	Toxics Use Reduction Institute
environmentalhealthnews.org	Environmental Health News
bchealthguide.org	British Columbia Health Guide
ehponline.org	Environmental Health Perspectives

Reference websites on TOXINS AND CHILDREN'S HEALTH ISSUES

healthychild.org	Healthy Child, Healthy World
childenvironment.org	Mt Sinai School of Medicine, Ctr Children's Health & Environment
cehn.org	Children's Environmental Health Network
preventingharm.org	Resource & Action Center on Children & the Environment
epa.gov/kidshometour	Teaches children about household toxins
epa.gov/envirohealth/children	America's Children and the Environment (ACE)
nrdc.org/breastmilk	Safer breast-feeding information; Reducing pollutants in breast milk
chem-tox.com	Research on chemicals, pesticides and health
safeminds.org	Sensible Action for Ending Mercury-Induced Neurological Disorders
ewg.org	Environmental Working Group
dienviro.com	The Deirdre Imus Environmental Center for Pediatric Oncology
ecomamas.com	Resource for parents who want to reduce toxins
iceh.org	Institute for Children's Environmental Health

General reference websites on TOXINS, CHEMICALS AND/OR HEALTHY LIVING

eartheasy.com	Safer options for clothing, diapers, food, cleaning, gardening, etc.
Home-SAFE-Home.org	Safer options for household products
healthandenvironment.org	Research updates on effects of toxins on health and environment
mindfully.org	Resource/links on many topics such as plastics & pesticides
thegreenguide.com	Product review, green home tips, environmental health updates
saferproducts.org	Clean Production Action
ehso.com	Environment, Health and Safety Online
care2.com/healthyliving	Healthy nontoxic living from cooking, personal care to pet care
responsibleshopper.org	Search of products/companies for safety updates
thenakedtruthproject.org	A resource for nontoxic living
pureknowhow.com	Practical solutions & skills for better health
chemicalbodyburden.org	Chemical body burden information; Coming Clean network

websites on DANGERS OF PESTICIDES AND FINDING SAFER ALTERNATIVES

pesticide.org	National Coalition for Alternatives to Pesticides (NCAP)
pesticides.org	Pesticide Education Center
epa.gov/pesticides	Environmental Protection Agency
protectingourhealth.org	The Collaborative on Health and the Environment
beyondpesticides.org	National Coalition Against the Misuse of Pesticides
chem-tox.com/cancerchildren	Research on pesticides, petrochemicals and cancer
foodnews.org	Pesticides in produce
mindfully.org	References on pesticides
healthychild.org	Healthy Child Healthy World
ewg.org	Environmental Working Group
pesticideinfo.org	Pesticide Action Network North America

websites on TOXINS IN SCHOOLS AND FINDING SAFER OPTIONS

chej.org	epa.gov/schools
childproofing.org	healthyschools.com
cleaningpro.com	healthyschools.org
edfacilities.org	informinc.org (see Cleaning for Health)

websites on TOXINS IN PERFUMES, SCENTS AND FRAGRANCES

www.ehnca.org
fpinva.org

websites that sell SAFER PRODUCTS:

These include personal care products, cleaning products, diapers, bedding, baby bottles, clothing, etc. Always read product information to ensure safer ingredients/materials.

absolutelyorganicbaby.com
abundantearth.com
adiri.com (baby bottles)*
babyminestore.com
beanproducts.com
bellysprout.com
childorganics.com
cloth-diaper.com
diapersafari.com
earthybirthymama.com
eartheasy.com
ecobaby.com
ecogoods.com
ecomall.com
ethicbaby.com
gogreenisland.com
goodhumans.com
greenfeet.com
greenforbaby.com
greenmatters.com
greennest.com
greentogrow.com (baby bottles)*
growinguporganic.ca
happyhealthybaby.com

lifekind.com
healthgoods.com
healthygreengoods.com
lilysgardenherbals.com
maggiespureland.com
mostnaturally.com
naturalebaby.com
natural-beds-pillows.com
natural-lifestyle.com
naturescrib.com
newbornfree.com (baby bottles & sippy cups)*
newenglandnatural.com
nontoxic.com
organicgrace.com
ourgreenhouse.com
purebeginnings.com
purehomeproducts.com
sagecreeknaturals.com
shopnatural.com
theconsciouschild.com
tinytush.com
vedababy.com
vermontsoap.com
ziaandtia.com

* made from plastics free of bisphenol-A (BPA) and phthalates; see websites for names of these plastics

websites with SAFER MAKE-UP and/or make-up ingredients to avoid

beautywithacause.com
lavera-usa.com
realpurity.com
cosmeticsdatabase.com

nottoopretty.org
onegrp.com
organicmakeup.ca
safecosmetics.org

websites with SAFER PERSONAL CARE PRODUCTS at a DISCOUNT

smartbomb.com
drugstore.com

vitacost.com
vitaminshoppe.com

COMPANIES WITH SAFER BABY PERSONAL CARE PRODUCTS

These are just a few of the many companies who make safer products, using natural ingredients. As always, it's up to you to CHECK THE INGREDIENTS carefully regardless of product or brand to ensure safety.

Aubrey Organics® (aubrey-organics.com)
Aunt Ann's Soaps (auntannsgardensoap.com)
Badger® (badgerbalm.com)
Beeswork® (beeswork.com)
Country Comfort® (natural baby care)
Dr. Bronner's® (drbronner.com)
Earth Mama Angel Baby®
    (earthmamaangelbaby.com)

Herbs for Kids® (herbsforkids.com)
Seventh Generation®
    baby wipes (seventhgeneration.com)
Tender Care® (tendercarediapers.com)
Terressentials® (terressentials.com)
un-petroleum Multi-Purpose Jelly®
    (unpetroleum.com)
Weleda® (weleda.com)

WEBSITES AND COMPANIES WITH SAFER TOYS

These include wooden toys and those made of organic materials. Search the websites (and if necessary call the companies) for guarantees that their non-toxic, natural products are free of PVCs, bisphenol-A, phthalates, flame-retardants, lead, mercury, etc.

For updates on toy safety:
    toysafety.net, uspirg.org, responsibleshopper.org, recalls.gov, cpsc.gov, healthytoys.org

bellysprout.com
ecomall.com/biz/toys.htm
kidbean.com
learningmaterialswork.com
learningwithtoys.com
naturaleco.com
naturalplay.com
naturescrib.com
organicgrace.com
organictoybox.com
ourgreenhouse.com
playstoretoys.com
purehomeproducts.com
sumboshine.com
tinybirdsorganics.com
turnertoys.com
ziaandtia.com

See also: Online web directories listed on page 65 for list of web retailers that specialize in natural toys

COMPANIES WITH SAFER CLEANING PRODUCTS

Bon Ami® (bonami.com)
Dragonfly Organix™ (dragonflyorganix.com)
Dr. Bronner's® (drbronner.com)
Earth Friendly Cleaners® (ecos.com)
Ecover® (ecover.com)

EnviroSafe Inc® (envirosafeipm.com)
Life Tree® Products (lifetreeproducts.com)
Maggie's Soap Nuts™ (maggiespureland.com)
Nature Clean® Living (naturecleanliving.com)
Seventh Generation® (seventhgeneration.com)

COMPANIES/ONLINE STORES WITH SAFER PEST CONTROL PRODUCTS

All Terrain® Kids Herbal Armor Insect Repellent (DEET-free) (allterrainco.com)
Botanical Solutions, Inc. (botanicalsolutions.com) e.g., tick guard (DEET-free)
Bite Blocker® (homs.com) organic insect repellent
Earth Easy (eartheasy.com)
EnviroSafe, Inc. (envirosafeipm.com) Integrated Pest Management (IPM) products
Garden Guys™ (garden-guys.com) safer lawn, insect control and cleaning products
Lewey's Eco-Blends, Inc. (buzzoff.us) DEET-free, 100% natural insect repellent
NaturaLawn® of America (nl-amer.com)
North Country Organics (norganics.com)
Organic-Gro™ (organic-gro.com)
Pharm Solutions, Inc. (pharmsolutions.com) organic, non-toxic, pest control products
Safer® Brand (saferbrand.com) online store for safer options
Safe2use (safe2use.com) online store for safer options, resources, links
Safe Solutions, Inc. (safesolutionsinc.com)
Victor®, Poison-Free® Products, Concern®, Ringer® (woodstreamcorp.com)